TELL ME ABOUT WRITERS

ENID BLYTON

written by
Gillian Baverstock

Evans

Evans Brothers Limited

Enid Blyton Enid Blyton Enid Blyton

Published by Evans Brothers Limited
2A Portman Mansions
Chiltern Street
London W1M 1LE

© Evans Brothers Limited 1997
© in the text Enid Blyton Ltd
© in the design and series format Evans Brothers Ltd

First published 1997
Reprinted 1998

Printed by Graficas Reunidas SA, Spain

ISBN 0 237 51751 5

British Library Cataloguing in Publication data.
Baverstock, Gillian
    Tell me about Enid Blyton
    1. Blyton, Enid, 1898?-1968 - Juvenile literature 2. Women
    novelists, English - 20th century - Biography - Juvenile
    literature
    I. Title II. Enid Blyton
    823.9'12

Enid Blyton wrote more than 700 books for children. Enid was my mother. Let me tell you about her.

Enid was born in London in 1897, one hundred years ago. Her parents Thomas and Theresa had just moved from Sheffield. Thomas loved baby Enid very much. Once, he held her in his arms all night when she nearly died of whooping cough. In the morning she was much better.

Baby Enid

Enid Blyton standing in front of some of the books she wrote

The Blyton family soon moved to Beckenham in Kent. Here, Enid's two brothers, Hanly and Carey were born. Enid hated looking after her little brothers and helping her mother in the house. She spent all the time she could with her father.

Enid aged seven

The house in Beckenham where the Blyton family lived

Enid's father
Thomas

They worked in the garden together and went for long walks in the woods and fields. Enid loved to read and her father gave her lots of books. A favourite book was "Alice in Wonderland" by Lewis Carroll. When she was older, she read all her father's books, even his encyclopedias.

Beckenham looked like this when Enid Blyton lived there.

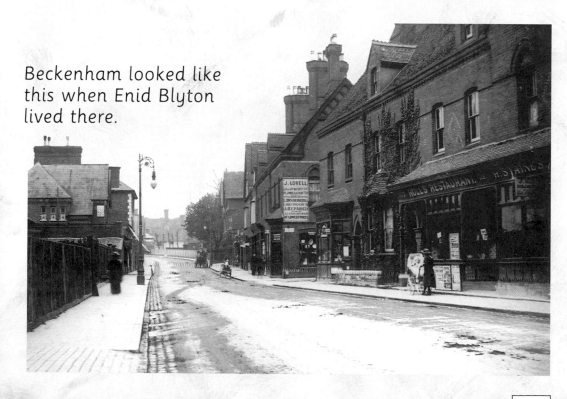

Enid's father left home when she was thirteen. He had been her best friend and she missed him very much. Now she was only really happy at school. Sometimes she got into trouble for playing tricks in class. She and her friends had fun writing to each other in code.

Enid played lacrosse at school. She was very good at games and English but she hated maths.

A letter in code from Enid to a friend

St Christopher's School in Beckenham, where Enid was a pupil

The book of poems that Enid's mother gave her

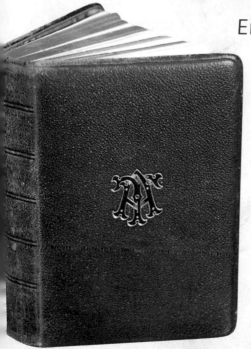

Enid liked writing. She wrote little plays and songs for school concerts. When she was fourteen she won a poetry competition. She wrote stories and sent them to magazines, but no one wanted to print them. Her mother was cross because she thought Enid was wasting her time, but she did give Enid a book of poems for her sixteenth birthday.

9

When Enid was nineteen, she left home to train as a teacher. She loved teaching, and in the holidays she could write her stories. In 1922 her first book was published. It was a book of poems called "Child Whispers". An old schoolfriend drew the picture for the cover.

Child Whispers
by
Enid Blyton

Copyright

J. SAVILLE & Co.
EDUCATIONAL PUBLISHERS
5, Gower Street,
LONDON, W.C. 1.

2/6 nett

PHYLLIS
CHASE

The cover of Enid Blyton's first book

Enid Blyton with her first pupils

10

Two years later, Enid married a publisher called Hugh Pollock. Enid stopped teaching and worked for a teachers' magazine. The teachers read her stories to their classes and lots of children wrote to her. Often there were so many letters she could not answer them all. So she put money in her collecting box for Great Ormond Street Hospital instead.

Enid and Hugh on their wedding day

She also wrote a little magazine called "Sunny Stories". She was so busy she had to learn to type.

GETTING WELL
THANK YOU
THE HOSPITAL FOR SICK CHILDREN.
GREAT ORMOND ST. LONDON, W.C.I.

Enid had a collecting box like this one

THE LONDON BOROUGH OF BROMLEY
ENID BLYTON
1897 – 1968
AUTHORESS
lived here

This plaque is now on the front of Elfin Cottage (right)

Enid Blyton loved gardening.

Enid and Hugh lived in a house called Elfin Cottage. They turned a field into a beautiful garden. Afterwards she wrote a book called "Let's garden". When I was little I was cross because my mother would not let me build a pond, although her book told me exactly how to do it!

Old Thatch today

In 1929 Enid and Hugh moved to Old Thatch. This is where I was born. My sister Imogen was born four years later.

In the evenings, when nanny took baby Imogen for her bath, Enid read me the stories she had written that day. She even made up stories about my doll, Amelia Jane, who was very naughty!

Amelia Jane

13

I loved being with my mother. We often walked down the lane and along the river with the dogs.

When Enid was little she was not allowed to have pets. Once she found a lost kitten, but her mother gave it away. So now she had lots of pets - two terriers, three Siamese cats, pigeons, doves, a tortoise, goldfish and some hens!

One of Enid's dogs

Enid gives me a hug because I am frightened of the lambs!

14

Enid Blyton at work at Green Hedges

One of the books Enid wrote at Green Hedges

THE MAGIC FARAWAY TREE BY ENID BLYTON

In 1938 we moved to a bigger house, called Green Hedges. Enid Blyton wrote all her well-known books here.

My favourite book was "Secret Island". In it, the children build a house of willow branches which start to grow. I planted a willow twig to see it if would really grow. It did - into an enormous tree!

15

The Second World War began in 1939. During the war Enid's first marriage ended, and she married a doctor. We all went on holidays together to the seaside in Dorset. After one holiday there, she wrote the first Famous Five book, "Five on a Treasure Island".

Enid's daughters, Gillian and Imogen

In wartime, paper for printing books was very hard to get. "Mary Mouse" was printed on paper strips left over from another book.

MARY MOUSE AND THE **GARDEN PARTY** IMAGINED BY **ENID BLYTON**

One of Enid Blyton's cartoon stories, printed on leftover paper

FIVE ON A TREASURE ISLA *Enid Blyton*

H&S

After the war Enid met a Dutch artist called Harmsen Van Der Beek. He painted brightly coloured little people. Enid loved his pictures. She asked him to paint the pictures for her next book. That week, Enid wrote the first two Noddy books.

Noddy and Big Ears, painted by Van Der Beek

A model of Noddy

17

Enid became busier than ever. In the next ten years she wrote two hundred books, a Noddy pantomime, two Famous Five films and a play.

She ran four clubs through the new "Enid Blyton's Magazine". Children who joined the clubs collected money to help children in need.

Children from all over the world wrote to her. She read every letter and tried to answer each one.

A scene from a new Famous Five television programme

Enid Blyton could write a book in a week. She sat down with her typewriter and closed her eyes. After a few minutes, children came into her mind, laughing and talking. She saw the places where everything would happen. Then the story filled her mind and she wrote it down as fast as she could.

Enid and her husband Kenneth look at a new story

Enid Blyton checks her latest book at the printers.

Enid kept on writing until she became ill. She died in 1968, when she was seventy-one years old. She always loved talking to children and telling them stories. Today children still love to read her stories, and watch films of her books.

Children from all over the world wrote to their favourite author, Enid Blyton.

Important dates

1897 Enid Blyton was born
1907 She went to St. Christopher's School for Girls
       in Beckenham
1910 Her father left home
1916 Started at teacher training college
1919 First teaching job in Bickley, Kent
1922 Her first book "Child Whispers" was published
1924 Married Hugh Pollock
1926 Moved to Elfin Cottage
1929 Moved to Old Thatch
1931 First daughter Gillian born
1935 Second daughter Imogen born
1938 Moved to Green Hedges;
      "The Secret Island" published
1942 First Famous Five novel published;
      divorced Hugh Pollock
1943 Married Kenneth Darrell Waters
1949 Met artist Van Der Beek; "Little
      Noddy Goes to Toyland" published;
      First Secret Seven book published
1967 Kenneth Darrell Waters died
1968 Enid Blyton died

Enid Blyton's favourite garden statue. A silver model
of it called the Enid Blyton Award is to be given each
year to someone who has helped children.

Keywords

artist
someone who makes
drawings and paintings

encyclopedia
a book or series of books
with information on many
subjects, arranged in
alphabetical order

magazine
like a book with pictures,
which is published regularly

publisher
someone who produces
books or magazines for sale

Index

"Child Whispers" 10

Dorset 16

Famous Five 16, 18, 20
films 20

Green Hedges 15

London 5
"Let's Garden" 12

magazines 9, 11
Mary Mouse 16

Noddy 17, 18

Old Thatch 13

pets 14
printer 19
publisher 11

school 8, 9
Sheffield 5

teaching 10, 11
Theresa, Enid's mother 5, 9
Thomas, Enid's father 5, 6, 7, 18

Van Der Beek, Harmsen 17

War, Second World 16, 17